Franklin's Passage

The Hugh MacLennan Poetry Series

Editors: Kerry McSweeney and Joan Harcourt
Selection Committee: Donald H. Akenson, Philip Cercone,
Allan Hepburn, and Carolyn Smart

TITLES IN THE SERIES

Franklin's Passage

David Solway

McGill-Queen's University Press

Montreal & Kingston · London · Ithaca

© David Solway 2003
ISBN 0-7735-2683-8

Legal deposit third quarter 2003
Bibliothèque nationale du Québec

Printed in Canada on acid-free paper.

McGill-Queen's University Press acknowledges
the support of the Canada Council for the Arts
for our publishing program. We also acknowledge the
financial support of the Government of Canada through
the Book Publishing Industry Development Program
(BPIDP) for our publishing activities.

National Library of Canada Cataloguing in Publication

Solway, David, 1941–
    Franklin's passage/David Solway.
    (Hugh MacLennan poetry series; 13)
    Poems.
    ISBN 0-7735-2683-8
    I. Title. II. Series.
    PS8537.04F73 2003   C811'.54   C2003-903361-9

This book was typeset by Dynagram Inc.
in 9.5/13 New Baskerville.

for Hannah

CONTENTS

Caught – the bubble
in the spirit level,
a creature divided;
and the compass needle
wobbling and wavering,
undecided.

                    Elizabeth Bishop, "Sonnet"

They've sailed east and they've sailed west
Round Greenland's coast they knew their best
In hardships they vainly strove
On mountains of ice their ships were drove
                                    Anonymous

How could they know, even stand back and see
The nature of the place they stood on,
When no man can, no man knows where he stands
Until he leaves his place, looks back
and knows.

            Gwendoyln MacEwen, *Terror and Erebus*

Is not our own interior white on the chart? Is it a North-
West passage around this continent, that we would
find? Are these the problems which most concern man-
kind? Is Franklin the only man who is lost?

                    Henry David Thoreau, *Walden*

DEDICATORY

We voyage as companions in ships there's
no way to abandon or desert – on
authority of Mowat and Berton
who chart our encounters with the weathers
that beset the soul. Woodman and Beattie,
Cookman and McGoogan affirm as well
how we must traffic with the layered swell
of wave and ice that resist entreaty.
One way or another we are stuck here,
clenched in the dream that drove us far from home
to confront the narratives we've come from
and try to make asymmetries cohere.
This is what a serious thinker says.
(Not Jean Baudrillard but Barry Lopez.)

This is a story
beyond the imagination
of the present moment.

He knows
he must keep
the narrative going,

stamp
his familiar prints
on a blank surface,

codifying
a brief flourish
of avens and lupines

into something
decipherable,
a legible report.

He knows
he must keep
speaking for the sound,

reciting
the litany
of wind and ice

that moans
about his ears,
grinds beneath his feet.

Skilled
in precipitous transitions,
he knows

when the story
stops, everything
stops.

Left behind in the pinnace,
five bibles
and *The Vicar of Wakefield.*

It's also about the land, di-
vided up any number of ways,
boulders, islands, strata, tracts,
their subsidence and resurgence;

about the pilgrimage across
these buckling peripheries,
the voyage and the quest
a chronicle apart,

yet meant to diffract
a serial event,
a sequence of acts
linked to a dark serendipity.

It's about a forced passage
beyond the timber line
which, as always, becomes
an absolute breach

like a line incised in stone
or drawn in ink
across the bottom of a page
or a word spoken *in extremis.*

It's about the broken track
one must follow
in this drift of encompassing silence,
turning the needle to ice.

We set out
in good weather
and the best of spirits,

confident,
knowing the danger
yet underestimating it,

the sheer magnitude of
the task, the sea, the land,
and the crystal amalgam of all these,

bulk ice –
which finally closed off our retreat
as it did our slow advance,

its only gift
a watery viaticum of rum.
Delirium drove us south

away from the whales in the channel,
while sniper lead picked off
those pneumonia had spared.

We thought the ice
an unscaleable wall
but were, once more, mistaken –

lichen trailing
creepers of gunpowder
into the fissures.

I bequeath this revelation
to all who shall come after.
Ice is the Northwest Passage,

our navigable route
to the distant coast,
land of shadow and cold.

You can't eat saxifrage and harebells.
Rock tripe, laver and shoreside kelp
are locked in pack ice.
Dog lichen and moss steeped in melted brash
make an inedible gruel
though an excellent glue for caulking.
Old rope feazed into oakum doesn't chew.
To take our minds off Goldner's tins
we holystone the planks with blocks of hematite
heavy as lumps of demerara,
scour the corners with bible-stones.
We keep the ship clean
for the lady in the long white dress
who comes with empty hands from the orlop deck
and leads us one by one into her bed.

from the journal of James Fitzjames, Captain of the Erebus

"I hope the lack of light is our most serious worry," the Commander said to us today. "The sun has bidden us farewell and now we face the wintry darkness." But there is light in abundance. Above us shines Polaris, the yellowish star that never seems to move, trapped in the black ice of the night sky. The lesser lights of the Great Bear prowl round it as if hunting for sustenance. Aurora Borealis, whose billowy green and rose-coloured banners stream and undulate across the dark backdrop of our *mise-en-scène*, are like the torches of the dead that light the living in their troubled passage to an obscure destination. The moon in its sconce of cloud is a harbinger of alien beauty. Here within, the small flames flicker on their slender wicks casting tremulous shadows on the narrow walls of the cabin like broken semaphores. Their message is clear nevertheless. I strike a match to fire the little coal of tobacco in the bowl, this and the tallow-illumined page with its hard and unintended clarities my last and only consolations. And yet when I reflect I see it may not be so and that these are lusters I could easily relinquish despite their ambiguous comfort. Light is always fickle and beauty does not console for it is founded in dread.

The German novelist saw him differently –
not as the dull and lethargic signals officer
who just happened to be at Trafalgar,
too dim-witted to panic in the calyx of fire,
passed over for promotion,
pensioned on half pay,
reduced to the governorship of a prison colony,
a methodical legalist who assumed too much,
a man with a gift for turning
a career into a cannonball's trajectory,
the Admiralty's *fourth* choice to lead the Expedition;
nor as the man who earlier had coasted
the shoreline of Bathurst Inlet
at the cost of half his men, duly lost
to starvation, murder and poor decision-making,
yet who found his consolation in
three squares *per diem* and innumerable cups of tea.
The German novelist saw him differently –
as a man given to the rhythms of reflection,
measured, contemplative, leisurely,
a man so far ahead of his time as to seem retarded,
who overlooked the fragmentary event
in favour of the wholeness of things,
who dug down deep into the structure of things
beneath the world's accelerated fever,

exploring the groundwork of system and pattern,
a paradigm for any age,
as the man who missed the Passage by a winter
but made *The Discovery of Slowness.*

Dear D.S.

That's not how it was. Trust me.
My three-year trek through the archives
has made it glaringly obvious
Franklin was the wrong man for the job.
Fatuous, overweight, slovenly, bovine;
aproned to his wife's ambitions –
Oh but that Lady Franklin was a piece of work,
a block of calculating ice –;
Franklin himself just piecework;
as a mariner, incompetent;
as a judge of situations, a veritable imbecile;
as a man, indecisive;
as a leader of men, lethal.
The Expedition was lost before it left Stromness.
Disko was a mere formality,
Lancaster Sound the devil's vestibule.
You get a sense of it in Cresswell:
a team of strung-out crew
sledging over hummocky ice,
manhauling a dwindling cache of provisions
through those glacial portals into the frozen circle –
the Arctic or the Ninth, same difference –
"forging the last link with their lives"

(the sound bite of the day).

That, my friend, was Franklin's doing.

And then they gave him credit for the Passage.

K.M.

Whereas the claimant of the second part
has served notice to the Claimant of the first part
that the latter should forthwith pursue
a pressing and magnanimous interest
in the subject of recovery and deliverance,

the Claimant of the first part
shall herewith and in condign regard
of the mutual covenants and agreements
herein and elsewhere stipulated
ratify the subject as specified above.

Once such commitments have been identified,
especially on the part of the Claimant of the first part,
the claimant of the second part
will ascertain a convenable date
for due consideration of the Claimant of the first part.

Both parties will ensure
that should a suitable convergence be arrived at
the Claimant of the first part
shall execute this agreement
with care and keen desire.

Each party to this indenture will herewith confirm
that the foregoing and the forthcoming
has and will be entered into
with solicitude for one another's natures,

whether patient or exigent,
impulsive or long-suffering.
In witness whereof
the claimant of the second part
awaits with appropriate restraint and confidence
the prospect of both parties
setting their respective seals on one another.

Cairned June 11, 1847, near Felix Point
John Franklin

We trace identical descent,
    the astronaut, the diver
and the explorer in his tent,
    by land or sky or river,

whether given to adventure
    or the antiquary craft,
in liberty or indenture,
    by boat or boot, sledge or raft,

whether peasant-born or gentry,
    the sailor or the marcher,
whether burning on re-entry
    or freezing at departure.

John Franklin, circa 2003

I am walking in the direction
in which I am walking
or I am walking away from it –
there is no way to tell.
Views and angles, like bits of broken glass in a tube, shift,
segments move, shards glitter, change, dissolve,
soon all is reduced
to iceblink and whiteout, disorienting my steps,
the coastal plurals of recollection
shrink to a single, low, undifferentiated plateau.
All directions are the same now.
In this land, deception is no more
feasible than salvation.
Is it possible that once we walked
on the downs by the Thames at Greenhithe?
I am walking into the snow
that blinds the eye and makes everything clear.
Dearest Elizabeth, far too late, I now confess
that I have always loved you
although you are my brother's wife
and I have ever walked beside you circumspectly.

As the Twin Otter
bearing the instruments
of his resurrection
banks and settles
to the ice,

rale of wind vibrates
in the sonic hum of the receiver.
Boots crunch on snow,
hatchets, shovels
ring against the stone.

Cautious hands
dislodge the coffin
wedged in glacier-rock,
lever it to the surface,
noisily pry off the lid.

They sprinkle and lave
warm water
like a benediction
over his winding-sheet of ice.
They cannot suppress an exclamation!

The dead man looks up
and stares at his interpreters,
head cocked to one side
as if listening for the sound
that no one else can hear.

They open the body
carefully
beneath the inverted y-incision
of a prior autopsy,

an earlier surgeon
sounding the depths
of the coiling infected viscera,
dissecting the long eel.

Probing gently
in the dark body of death
they cut out samples
for the lab,

then reel the gut
down into its mummy pit,
stitching the frayed edges
of the vent together.

They settle him back
into his boat
and lower it again
into that shallow, ice-packed sea.

He was a tall man for his time,
"just under six feet," the narrator,
a stranger to irony, says.
The coffin was a tight fit.
They had to tuck the left arm
under the body,
raise the knees slightly.
Even more puzzling,
the signs of an earlier autopsy,
organs tossed back helter-skelter
into the abdominal cavity.
Assessing data, exhuming reasons,
piecing together the story line,
lead solder sealing the competing plot,
they opt for pneumonia and madness.
As usual they get it wrong.
Or anyway, half wrong.

Received in the mail,
January 9, 2003,
a complimentary copy
of Paul Illidge's novel *Shore*.
The book falls open to page 94
and discloses its message:

IN MEMORIAM
Captain Franklin Barnes Shore 1908–1958
Elizabeth Warren Shore 1921–1959
"winnetoon pendeek noochimmoin marchian"
"Lost In Life's Hard Journey"

– What's the idea? Jonathan asks uncertainly.

What's the idea?
As we cross the meridians
dividing one shore from another
in the kingdom of contingency,
this is bound to keep happening.

These were found assembled in the cairn
paired as if for company:

a silver crucifix
and a coil of chafed hemp;
the object glass of a marine telescope,
flinders of coal;
two gilt buttons,
one stamped with an anchor,
the other with a crown;
a colored silk handkerchief laid beside
orts of coarsely sewn canvas;
a medicine chest and the haft of an oar;
finally, several muskets in a cromlech ring
circling a message hastily scrawled
on the torn page of a muster book.
Sir James Ross' pillar has not however been found
and the paper has been transferred to this position
which is that in which Sir J. Ross' pillar was erected.

The cache is partially intelligible.
The message makes no sense to anyone.

They would gladly have traded the Passage
for a little ship's biscuit,
a hogshead of ale,
a few strings of salt horse
and a firkin of hard lard.
They would joyfully have foregone
the ceremony of departures and arrivals
for a mat of salted cod,
a handful of raisins in suet
or a keg of pickled cranberries.
A kettle of iron soup laced with parsnips
would have deputized for the Eucharist
and a carrot of tobacco bound in twine
for the monstrance.
Would that the box stuffed with hymnals
had been a crate of Normandy pippins.
Lord, cascade them with apples and pears
for a bill of provisions is an empty promise
and words do not sustain us in extremity.

We eat what is in the tins.
Something eats into our bones,
eats, eats,
as rats gnaw at the corpses in the hold.
(Soon we will eat the rats.)
Ice surrounds and devours the ship.
Ice eats rock, wood, earth.
Ice eats men.
(Soon we will eat the ice.)

Look here.
The X-ray of the skull
yields no detail.
The cranium is filled with ice.

The Utjulik Report

What they found using
the Scintrex Smartmag 4 portable cesium magnetometer
didn't amount to very much,
and the Knudsen 320A through-ice echo sounder,
even less.
The survey map is detailed, impressive and authoritative
though yielding little in the way of results
except to confirm that neither
Erebus nor *Terror*
reposed in their projected locations
somewhere between Grant Point and Kirkwall Island,
under the crisscrossing skidoos.
Perhaps Inuit testimony is unreliable.
Perhaps expert methodology is unreliable.
But failing the dredging of graphic evidence
tracking the wreck of human enterprise,
we can always photograph ourselves
surrounded by the gear of accessory exploits,
ruddy and smiling in our parkas.
We can always tell another story
leaning companionably into the sun.

Someone sewed this odd-man-out button
into the strong fabric
to batten down the body's heat
and keep out the cold,
never imagining the real story.
It kept *in* the cold,
bundled the cold
deep inside the blue, thick-ply cerements,
kept the cold warm and living
to accomplish its ordained purpose
of devouring from within,
severing word from speech,
voice from word,
the cry of supplication from breath itself,
shaping the frozen syntax of the North.

It is a thing in itself, the cold,
a creature rising from below the threshhold
of human consciousness
or descending from above the spirit level,
tracked by the mercury until the mercury freezes
solid in its bulb and cylinder,
sensed in the extremities until sense is numbed,
stalking everywhere and invisibly,
palpable, relentless, bulletproof, famished,
consuming what little is left of light,
biting to the bone of darkness.
It cannot be domesticated or hunted down.
It resists the illusion of measurement.
It is not the absence of warmth.
It is a thing in itself, the cold.

Now they know.
Or think they know.
The Northwest Passage
was surely in the air.
Ice was meant to fly over,
the Twin Otter threading
north and south together
like the lappets of a shroud.

We know differently.
Ice is meant to be grappled with,
broken through,
trudged over,
listened to,
died on.

We know this, too.
The Northwest Passage
is where it always was.
It is here right beneath our feet.

When the wind dropped
and our vision cleared
we thought we might get our bearings
but were, as usual, wrong.
The storm resumed
and I recalled a distant celebration
in a lit room
in which we read the tale of our salvation
cheered by puddings and mulled wine,
the sound of fiddles and bells
healing for a time
the lesion in the middle of our lives.
The world is now bare,
unbedecked as the back of a Christmas tree,
no gifts to open,
the grinterns empty,
nothing to give thanks for
but this sudden and unexpected
illumination.

They must have decided
to return to the ship
despite the flaming sword
of the never-setting, the dark sword
of the never-rising, sun.
Same old story.
The way back into the garden
is also the way
into the realm of the minerals.
In the end
what we are looking for
will find us.
"Living must be your whole occupation,"
the poet wrote. He got it right.
No, he got it half right.

For the French philosopher the world is uncertain
because it cannot be exchanged for anything else
nor can thought be exchanged for truth or the Real –
neither one nor the other has an equivalent anywhere –
and because our ships are beset by a frozen consilience
we are trapped in a system of impossible exchanges,
the Northwest Passage ineluctably choked
by the towering floes of nontransitivity.
Of course, the French philosopher is impossibly French
and has never observed the beauty of the nunataks
or watched the wind stirring in the leaves of the dwarf birch
or imagined trading in the markets of the North
exchanging iron and wood for blubber and meat
and tales of conquest for myths of creation
or set his ear gingerly against the fret of a paddle
hearing the tremolo of the singing whale
or hiked across tundra with a pack on his back
to chart the terrain and dimensions of the possible.

They come in all forms
and different orders of magnitude:
pocket-sized, framed in cherrywood,
giving back the common lineament;
the tropic device of thickened panes
painted with sooty translucence
and the frost of approximate discernment;
sheets of ice rising shear and stark
to startle with a long-forgotten shape
in the sunlit, unaccustomed night
of alien latitudes;
even the sky with its polished tain of cloud
assembles a ghostly embodiment
and lamps the visceral pitch of design.
But the voyage itself is the truest glass.
Scoured of flaws, smoke and biases,
it peels back the skin of the customary
to reflect an interior figure
vaguely intuited and routinely misconceived,
like a ship's completed manifest
accounting for the arc of discovery and loss
and bearing us back, astonished, to ourselves.

Don't be alarmed or skeptical –
you are only seeing what lies hidden
beyond your sightlines:
islands, mountains, lakes, coastlines, icebergs, ships
rising in perfect gradients,
strict metaphors of themselves,
reversed, inverted, identical,
these shimmering palisades seen through earth's blue haze
miming what lies beyond
the cambered deck of your vantage,
behind the half-moon of the horizon,
peaks and clefts, the natural play of reflection,
images pegged in air.
You are seeing what is called a "superior mirage."
You are reading precise analogies of what is there.

The film is called *Lost Voyage*.
According to the description
on the back of the box,
the story goes something like this.

Fascinated by things inexplicable and a prey to curiosity, Judd Nelson sets out to tackle the unexplained occurrences in the Bermuda Triangle. One of the Triangle's most intriguing victims, the cruise ship Corona Queen, suddenly emerges after a disappearance of more than 25 years. After learning of the ship's reappearance, his curiosity gets the better of him. Regardless of strange supernatural warnings, he joins a paranormal exploration team in the hope of accounting for the mysterious phenomenon. Once on board, they find the Corona Queen coming to life as they face horrifying unearthly forces.

The end of the tale will startle and astonish and leave you gasping for breath as you ponder its implications. The terror you will meet here is based on a true story.

What the summary doesn't say is
we are always at least one chronicle from the truth.

In the pavilions of the Lord, there will be much rejoicing:
the vine, and the fig, and the pomegranate, and the olive tree
shall all bring forth.
Here, at Cape Riley in the southwest corner of Devon Island,
only the debris of a stone hut
and a torn scrap of paper bearing the words:
until called.
The two epitaphs on the lonely graves across the causeway
    continue to puzzle.
As for the imaginary Croker Mountains closing off Lancaster
    Sound,
they might just as well have risen overnight
considering the river of ice permanently blocking the channel
down from the Beaufort Sea to abut at Victory Point.
Edom shuts its gates. Why continue to jib and swerve?
In the courtyard of the Lord, there is the foundation of the
    temple.
Here on the bare garrigue of Devon, waste and relic-strewn,
the stones tumble to the ground and lie about in disarray.
Who is left among you who saw this house in her first glory?
Thus saith the Lord of Hosts, consider your ways.
Choose ye this day whom ye will serve.

It's the skulls that bring it home,
give scale, give scope to it:
some with holes bored
into the intimate slope of bone
for the siphon's probing insertion;
some scooped out through the delicate auricles;
some poked and reamed through the eyes;
some split like crockery,
the shards scraped clean with rasps and hunting knives;
others with the jaws wedged off –
the best way to get at the brains;
and others still with their bowls intact,
arrayed on shelves of ice,
stacked in hutches of granite,
crated in boxes,
as if ready even now
to be drunk and eaten from.

The words are fitted
gingerly into place,
lifted up carefully, set
cheek by jowl together,
slotted and chinked,
the spaces plugged
with a grout of particles
or left intact as tiny
windows to see the sky
through, raised on a white
scarp or headland or ridge
like a pillar of fragments
calling attention to its
silent annexing presence,
its eloquent vigilance,
or like a low tower, a rebus
spelling out error and despair,
to be pried apart for the
message it encloses,
the message stored some
where in its chambered interior,
names broken up and reassembled,
the plea disguised as transcript,
tragedy presenting itself as information.

To reach the waters that opened suddenly
"not twenty feet from the bow"
and prevent the hull from being nipped
they had to cut a channel to the nearest lead,
chop two holes in the ice with axes,
rope the twelve-foot ice-saws to pulleys
lashed to makeshift tripods of ship's spars,
work the sawteeth through the holes,
crop the big blocks of ice to each side or shove them under,
then haul the ships zigzag through the snaking rivulets,
slowly breaching the pack between Devon and Cornwallis.

As for us, we do not use such rough-bladed saws.
We try to keep a distance,
to stay this side of the crack in the ice,
this side of Devon and Cornwallis,
in part out of tact,
in part because we cut and haul
along a different Passage.

Ask yourself these questions.

- Do you have experience in wilderness travel?
- Do you have the medical and survival skills required for self-reliance?
- Do you *have* self-reliance?
- Have you brought the necessary camping tackle, maps, safety equipment, first aid and repair kits?
- Are you familiar with bracing, maneuvering, surf launching and self-rescue techniques?
- Can you travel on a bearing and use triangulation to establish your position?
- Can you interpret marine charts and tide tables and use them to identify marine hazards?
- Can you navigate in fog?
- Do you possess a GPS unit for relaying accurate coordinates in case of disaster?
- Are you able to estimate current speeds and ferry angles?
- Do you have white water experience, canoe spray decks and wetsuits?
- Are you willing to wear Neoprene booties?
- Do you have judgment, forebearance and respect for changing conditions?
- Do you know what to do when the radio goes dead?
- Are you supplied with sufficient reserves of *quinuituq*?

- Are you sufficiently flexible to reassess at a moment's notice?
- Are you ready to deal with polar mirages?
- Do you have a passion for collecting spoons, knives, matchboxes, letter openers, squarehead nails, magnifying glasses, shako badges, compasses, medallions and chronometers?
- Do you have time and provisions for unexpected delays caused by bad weather, high water levels, icelock, cancelled shuttles and flights?
- Do you have alternate plans?
- Will you be traveling with others who have experience and training?
- Can you link tragedy to diversion?
- Do you have a tolerance for ongoing narratives which generally turn out to be the same narrative?
- Are you a good raconteur?
- Are you prepared to suffer all manner of indignities?
- Are you prepared to die?

The low granite hills
give way to woods
of white-barked birch
and weeping willow;
blue-green pine
and crimson-flowered larch
build cathedral arches
about our heads;
slips of bog rosemary
lace the ground
with their smoky tendrils;
rivers are silver-backed with fish.
This is our dream
of the south,
our dream of the opulent east,
only a few hundred miles away
in the north and west
of this sparse, extravagant land.

Madness, pneumonia, lead, cold,
more or less in that order.
It didn't stop there.
After cold, recognition,
terror and darkness,
the arch of transit,
landfall,
end without resolution,
one story telescoping into another,
then the luminous moment of understanding.

There is always a killer aboard.

And in our bones we understood
there was no eluding this assassin.
We could not
warp our ships through the pack
nor thread the blizzard
home to sanctuary.
We were soldered tight.

Now we know.
Genesis is haunted by Revelation.
And the Expedition
to the unpromising land
we undertook in the innocence of conviction
or the lust for ascendancy and place
is only the most elaborate
of our allegories.

the grave at Comfort Cove for who has any doubt how …

sting,   This is a message to the unimagined reader   *the*
set to embark on a voyage of exploration,
thy   searching for traces and clues of another journey   *dyer*
to a lateral destination
is   most likely missed or inconclusive   *sad …*
but without irreversible consequences.
whare We are safe within the margins of our purposes.
We need not try the drifts and pressure ridges,
scale limestone parapets rutted with snow
Death or slipe our baggage to some far, elusive haven
or boil tea in a house made of ice
to fuel the engines of our parable.
The flat expanse that hems our charting expedition in
Oh   yields a tepid consolation not to be discounted.
We can always reach across and put out the night.
We can always turn the page to other things.

*The words that frame this message were spelled backwards but restored
for the unimagined reader's convenience.*

How to explain
the missing plaque and fabric
from Hartnell's grave?

Set up a string grid,
prepare the X-ray slabs,
peg down the tent and seal the flaps,
stop the yellow leak of sunshine,
irradiate,
cut and stain the tissue,
preserve in a Petri dish,
sample and analyze,
publish your findings.

The question remains.
How to explain
the missing part of the story?

Possibly a massacre.
According to one version of events
among many other versions
of the same indeterminate event,
Crozier and his men were attacked by Inuit,
Crozier wounded, the men slaughtered,
the low hills of Ommanek chalky with skulls,
bones scattered helter skelter
like spilled compass needles
pointing in all directions
to the same tempting hypothesis,
stores rifled,
message cannisters pried open
and plundered of their coordinates,
truth disseminated
along ridges of limestone shingle
and rugged crushed-up pack
framing still another theatrical production.
Possibly a massacre.
Probably not.

"Wintered at Beechey Island
in Lat. 74–43'-28" N. Long. 90–39'-15" W.
after having ascended Wellington Channel to Lat. 77,
and returned by the west side of Cornwallis Island."

"And start on tomorrow, 26th, for Back's Fish River."

"Overland to the Great Piss-Pot by Pelly Bay,
then down to Chantrey Inlet
and across the flats to Cape Britannia."

"On the shore of the north side of the island
I found also an excavation
which I called a ship's trench,
dug out of stone,
which was of such a nature
as to yield to the persevering use
of pickaxe, sledge-hammer, and the crow bar.
From here they dragged the longboats down to Simpson Strait."

"When the wind dropped
and our vision cleared
we thought we might get our bearings."

"They cut across the Adelaide Peninsula
and wintered on O'Reilly Island.
Then they disappeared
over the vanes and stents of icy shale
into the endless archipelago of legend."

"'It was Aglooka the last Eshemuta
who saw the umiak sink beneath the ice.
He set off for Netsilak but found himself
wandering with his men in Tununeq.
This was what you call the back of beyond.'
Thus much has Artungun told me
as a man speaking
without any thought of deception."

"...ice impassable at Bellot Strait,
therefore south along the coast of Boothia
toward Erebus Bay,
eventually toward Thunder Cove,
then backtracked to the west
trending toward Crampton.
We may find them yet,
their movements hacked into the glacial archive,
their fate anchored in a small magnetic anomaly."

"The crest of the ridge was not very wide
and was formed of projecting rocks.
The slope was gradual but broken
by blades of boot-shredding gravel.
However,
the identification of the location
at Victory Point
is indeed persuasive."

"They traversed the Graham Gore Peninsula
where the mudstones gave way to meadows and lakes
and the rich hunting grounds of Cape Herschel,
but from there the transition
was truly an astounding one.
Save for a few taggers of discarded tin
they left no further traces,
swallowed by this desolate terrain."

"Hoping to make contact with the whalers
they laboured north to Somerset.
Their remains were committed to the shifting earth
to the west of Fury Beach,
their meager tombs eventually subsiding
into the viscous clay thrown up by the ponds,
marked only by tufts of purple saxifrage."

"The very light color of the *ar-nuk*
scattered here and there and frozen solid
made them think it could not be from Inuit,
which was of a dark appearance.
It seems possible, then, the Melville Peninsula
was a hunting ground for the Etkerlin
or more likely a home for the koblunas,
the surviving members of the Expedition."

"Needless to say, most of this was fantasy."

Sing them a ballad and tender their names:
Francis, Cornelius, Edmund and James,

Thomas and Graham and William and John
And another hundred and twenty were gone,

Charles and Robert and Henry and George,
To be martyred and purged in the wintry forge.

They set out to find the miraculous East
But were stalked by the weather and tracked by the beast.

The vessels were stoven by pressure and floe,
Then sunk to the bottom ten fathoms below

And those who escaped were ground bone by bone
In a mortar of ice by a pestle of stone.

Oh, victory comes in mysterious ways
And the men are all changed from their suffering clays,

Their spirits dissolved in the boreal mists,
Their names and their natures transformed into Christ's.

Every man is of course
an island entire of itself
though admittedly at times
a part of the Main.
But only at times.
Consider Beechey (see cover):
slate with a few scrawled names,
isolated and bleak,
an island fit for burials
under a hazy lamina of cloud,
sundered from the bigger mass of Devon
by drift ice and the sea's smalt chasm.
And yet in the proper season
when ice and sea recede
Beechey is briefly a peninsula
rawled by a narrow spit of gravel
barely four meters across
to the undiminished promontory
in which it is involved.
This would seem to provide
a kind of provisional evidence
for a stirring, initial hypothesis.
But consider as well that Devon,
the Main of which Beechey is an intermittent part,
is also an island.

Masts or spars distantly glimpsed off Maconochie Island;
wood chips with "Erebus" and "Mr. Stanley" scratched on them;
a black-painted strip of ship's block or the panel of a sea chest
studded with brass-headed tacks forming the initials I.F.[1]
(which Cyriax later determined matched no crewman's);
a missing document from a bottle at Cape Britannia and
   a 138 word record
plus a few scraps of paper found near Fury and Hecla Straits;
a tapered stone cross-piece on one cairn,
on another a wooden board carved as a pointing finger;
a pinewood pole rogue-yarned for signal halyards
and an oak stanchion turned on a wring lathe;
cask-slats and iron hoops, barrel staves and nameless planking
scattered on the track toward the Back River
leading through wrack-ice into the Barren Lands;
Mowat's "hardwood box with dovetailed corners" discovered at
   Angikuni Lake;
a few more relics: a sword, two tin kettles, a blunt pickaxe;
a tall dead man laid out in his bunk at Ootgoolik;
echoes of other expeditions confusing (or diversifying) the
   muniment;
the ever-shifting polar ice cap playing havoc with coordinates.
The *Arctic Pilot* also notes three cairns on Kirkwall Island

no one has troubled to consult – no doubt, to avoid anticlimax.
The message is clear:
little can be learned from what is called evidence.
Only the maps of past inadvertence,
only the stories, remain.

1 As the "I" was partially defaced,
   several tacks having possibly worked loose,
   Admiral Wright proposed "L.F." for Lieutenant
   (since, in the Royal Navy, Lieutenants were known as "Luffs"),
   Barr suggested "Lady Franklin,"
   the name of one of the sledges on another ship
   which may have drifted toward the northeast coast
   of O'Reilly Island in 1852,
   and Woodman came up with "R.I.P.",
   assuming a missing "R" and closing the "F,"
   referring to the dead man at Ootgoolik.

   Everything considered,
   might it not have been a "J"?

That was the year summer didn't come to the Arctic.
Our ships beset by ice,
crushed in the glacial jaws of its vice
north of King William Island,
we abandoned our once-unsinkable homes –
reinforced bomb-boats driven by locomotives
that could not budge the pack by an inch –
and trekked like solemn migratory wraiths
south toward the river and the fort,
pulling sleds filled with books and fine china,
leaving a pyramid of tins behind
to mark our passage to the underworld.
Exhaustion brought no peace,
conferred no balm of sleep or resignation
as we staggered in harness
tormented by the music of the elements
that tugged us toward the inevitable coast,
teased by an occasional patch of green –
rugs of sorrel, bladder campion, chickweed, stitchwort –
by sparse clumps of plumb-black crowberries
poking out of the hillside drifts,
driven by the red spurs of our own butchered flesh
that kept us going just long enough
to cross from one season into another,
to bridge the strait to the mainland

as far as Point Booth and Starvation Cove
where the last of us lay down together in the snow
and sank into the century without a trace.
That was the year summer didn't come to the Arctic,
the year we trudged into History
and not one of us lived to tell the tale.

This just in
direct from the kingdom of contingency.

Thank you for your order.
Abebooks has forwarded this order to the bookseller.
Frank Crowder Books.
Franklin, VA.
*The Franklin Conspiracy: Cover-up, betrayal, and the astonishing
    secret behind the lost Arctic Expedition.*
Jeffrey Blair Latta.
Payment processed by the Advanced Book Exchange.
Book description:
cover has rubbing and hint of stain,
spine sunned, edges foxed, label residue,
may have small remainder mark,
no dustjacket.
Second printing.
Approximate shipping speed: 21–36 business days.

Perhaps it is none of the usual suspects,
neither blizzard nor famine
nor beads of lead joining the seams
nor the infinite legions of *Clostridium*
nor an attack by the raw flesh eaters.
Perhaps there is another story to be told,
an alternate account to skew familiarity,
bring a new perspective to the glass –
the black ship riding on an iceberg
deep in the Northwest Triangle,
stately in its rigging,
wind eerie in the cordage,
emerging from the fog of weather and uncertainty,
glimpsed for a moment in the Sound
before vanishing again into the shrouds of winter
and the bounded circuit of the stars,
the men spirited by the Shaman's Light
into the regions of inference and presentiment,
their bones gnawed by the long-toothed Tunnit,
their memory betrayed by fact.
We should not be quick to discount our fictions.
There is always another story to be told.

He was among the first to die,
the progress of the illness undocumented,
the cause unascertained,
the Captain going down before his ship,
a desertion typically unintended.
No one knows where he was buried –
perhaps in the waters off Clarence Island
or in the icy coffin of King William's Land
or even on Matty Island's stone monotony.
No headboard has been found,
no record deposited in the cairns
that sentinel the scoured landscape,
no voices have been heard tacking the wind,
fording the Styx,
staking their allodial claim to the darkness.
A dozen expeditions have carded the North
for evidence of passage,
prolonging the narrative into sequels of conjecture,
skeining the vectors into likelihood.
Because the dead do not speak
except to themselves,
the legend of the end remains open-ended.
No one knows what accounted for his passing.
No one knows where his tomb reposes.

We must always distrust a "standard reconstruction."
It is likely our informant
confined his search to King William Island
and never crossed over to Starvation Cove,
so could not have found the boat there.
The boat was probably found later
on the islet in Douglas Bay
which further befuddled the teams of explorers
who thought it one of the Todds,
most likely Keeuna.
The clue lies in the one discordant element
in every explanation
or in the element that is lacking.
This is because the preponderance of evidence
is admittedly circumstantial
and the same boat tends to appear
in many different places.
Always look for where the bones are strewn,
root out the fact suppressed by decorum.
For the great tragedy of the Expedition
did not come at the end of the march
but in the middle
long before anyone arrived
at Keeuna or Starvation Cove.

Getting from here to there
is not as easy or convenable
as it may sound
despite the ice-master's discipline
and although it is needful for utterance
unless circumstance conspires
to open the leads
and fillet the channels of hamper and snag
and the pilgrim seizes on remoteness
alert to proximities of distance.

And depending on where
there happens to be.

In order to supplement a deficient record
the research team turned finally to the Ouija board.
It seemed the only way to breach that distant coast.
We summoned up the caulker's mate, still at his post
on *Erebus* trapped in antipodal weather –
the plectrum moving lightly as a feather
to spell a message out from there to here. It
seemed the quill-end of an unforgiving spirit
intent on rendering judgment, although too late.
The verdict it pronounced was ultimate.
"Old Sir John, I say he was a proper dunce.
He should have sailed down Peel Sound at once,
and not, as he was bidden, up the Wellington.
A solid Navy man, a slave to discipline."
The message ceased, but soon we felt the Pole
tug at the needle's point again. That restive soul
had one more thing to say to fill the crack
between assumption and event – what records lack –
before it sank into the dark the Ouija board
had briefly lit and lately steered us toward.
"It is night and winter here. We crave the sun.
May God be with you. My name was Francis Dunn."

The wave function rotates in Hilbert space
which is much like the Arctic,
an infinite-dimensional abstraction,
except that the Arctic kills
at specific times in localized coordinates.

Nevertheless, the Arctic is a world
describable by an evolving wave function
which contains within it a vast number
of radiating story lines,
continuously merging and branching.

For a teeming bunch of stories is
much simpler than any of its members.
In the same way, the set of all integers
may be generated far more readily
than a single number in its algorithmic string.

Yet each story is real and inescapable
in virtue of a process called decoherence
which mimics wave function collapse
while preserving unitarity.
Nothing is as random as it seems.

Of course, all possible initial conditions
coexist simultaneously
but taken in the icy clinch
decoherence causes them
to behave classically in separate braids and forks.

It is therefore no surprise,
no surprise at all,
whether in Hilbert space or in the Arctic,
that fluctuations in the plot
are strictly infinite and equally believable.

"But in the light gray, the indefinite, there we could live."

Lars Gustafsson, "Snow"

Over the trench and slab of longitude we make little headway.
There is too much glare to gauge where we are going.

In the featureless sumps of soft snow we fall to our knees
overwhelmed by a whiteness that obliterates everything.

The grainy air of blizzards does not constitute a panorama.
How can we be expected to take our bearings?

And when the wind dismantles the horizon and blows away the
    constellations
we are scattered like driftwood, like soapstone carvings, along
    the shore.

In the acetylene flare of the sun we are transfixed in place.
In the long darkness that closes over us we are wholly lost.

The moon reflects off basalt spires:
we are blinded with the strangeness of it.

But in the pale gleam of origins, the incipient, the heraldic
    light of early dawn,
there we could somehow persevere.

The narrative is fleshed
in many different ways
but its function remains the same,
to clothe the bones that lie beneath;

yet the bones themselves
are rarely intact
and must be recollected,
identified, numbered, docketed, stored.

There is not much to go on.
It all comes down to ice and shale
and a casting of words
accounting for nothing but recurrence.

We follow in imagination along uncharted routes,
keeping a distance from frazil and grease ice
and the treacherous film of young nilas
bending "like watered silk over a light ocean swell,"
avoiding the sharp spikes of needle ice at the bottom of melt
    pools,
listening for the tinkle of candle ice drained of brine,
testing gingerly the blue-tinted blocks of first-year ice
before it hardens into gray massifs of thick polar pack,
skirting the barbed edges of pancake ice that make walking
    difficult,
plotting circuits around hummocky ice and rubble ripraps
that swell into ridges making walking impossible, or next-to,
seeking unpredictable flaws in shorefast ice that open lanes of
    transit
and the glassy serenity of embayed ice, as shortlived as tempting,
always staying clear of the shifting rafts and masses of sea ice.

We do this by cutting transects from an altitude
or, keeping our feet on the ground,
by hobbling doggedly over the kerns and serifs of our passages.

CTV Wednesday night.
I turn up the sound.
Accompanied
by an ominous score,
David Suzuki on *The Nature of Things*
narrates the Franklin Expedition.
We are treated to broad, desolate, aerial views
of the island,
close-up exhumations,
the exploits of Forensic Anthropology.

In the same time slot
CBC presents another icy encounter
between the Pittsburg Penguins and the Red Army,
a serial event.
The organ in the loft plays triumphal music.
The crowd is going ballistic.

A creature divided,
I flip the channels effortlessly –
the breach not yet absolute –
collapsing distance into near-simultaneity
as I move from ice surface to ice surface,
achieving perfect passage
from one world to another,
keeping the story going.

ACKNOWLEDGMENTS

I wish to thank the Canada Council for the Arts for a writing grant which gave me the time to work on this collection.

Many excellent books on the Franklin expedition and related topics have appeared over the last decade or two. The Beattie/Geiger accounts, *Frozen In Time* and *Buried In Ice*, along with Ken McGoogan's recent *Fatal Passage*, provide the basis for continuing study. I am especially indebted to John Wilson's imaginative reconstruction of the journals of James Fitzjames, *North With Franklin,* and to David Woodman's analyses of the Inuit testimony, *Unravelling The Franklin Mystery* and *Strangers Among Us.* Scott Cookman's *Ice Blink* also provided much useful information. Two novels, *The Ice Child* by Elizabeth McGregor and *The Discovery of Slowness* by Sten Nadolny, make for fascinating reading as does Barry Lopez' extended meditation, *Arctic Dreams,* a veritable tour de force. I have also benefitted from Farley Mowat's *Walking On The Land* and *Ordeal By Ice* and from Pierre Berton's *Arctic Grail.* Jeffrey Blair Latta's radiological imaginings in *The Franklin Conspiracy* are nevertheless supported by an impressively close analysis of the paradoxes and discrepancies in the surviving documentation. Of interest also are the treatments accorded the Franklin narrative by several Canadian literary figures: Gwendolyn MacEwen's verse drama *Terror and Erebus,* Margaret Atwood's short story "The Age of Lead," and Mordecai Richler's expository passages in *Solomon*

Gursky Was Here. Finally, I have profited from an article in *Scientific American* on the subject of parallel universes which is central to my theme.

NOTE

For the sake of the unity and coherence of my own thematic reworking of these events, I have taken certain small liberties with the various conflicting accounts of John Franklin's calamitous attempt to find and map the Northwest Passage and of its aftermath, including as well the mysterious fate of his two ships, *Erebus* and *Terror.* I have on a number occasions incorporated brief passages of cannibalized text into the body of a given poem as part of the assembled materials. From time to time I have chosen place names with a view to appropriateness. For example, Starvation Cove was named by a later American exploratory team; it would have been known to Franklin as Richardson Point. Occasionally I have modified the documentary records, like the Inuit scavenging parties who found, broke up and put the wood of the Expedition's lifeboats to their own use. Some of these muniments have also had to be invented to suit my purposes.